COLORING
Book

_____

_____

_____

Test Your Colors Here

1968 Chevrolet Corvette Stingray

1965 Chevrolet Bel Air

1937 Bugatti Type 57

1940s GMC Pickup Hotrod

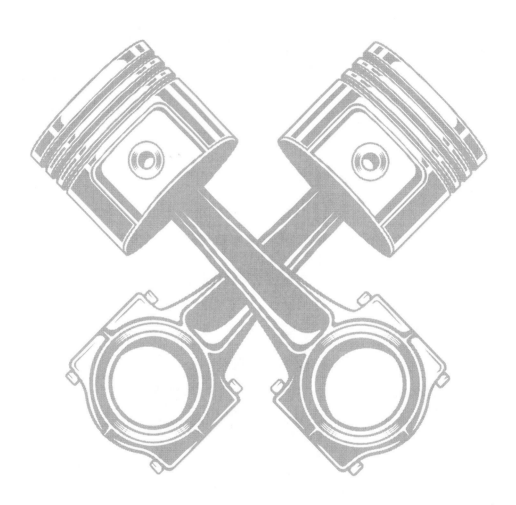

1939 GMC 100

1971 Chevrolet Suburban

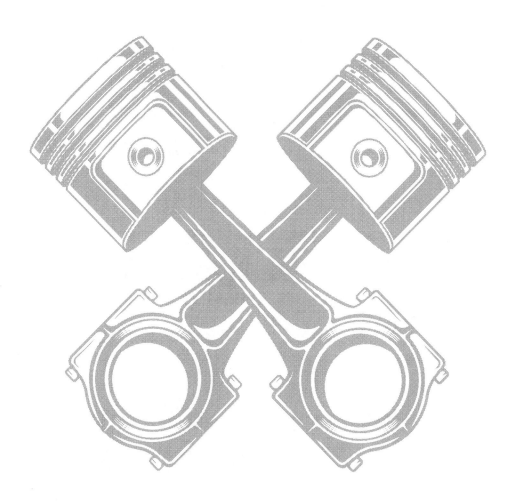

1968 Chevrolet C10

1963 Ferrari 250 GTO

1964 Oldsmobile 442

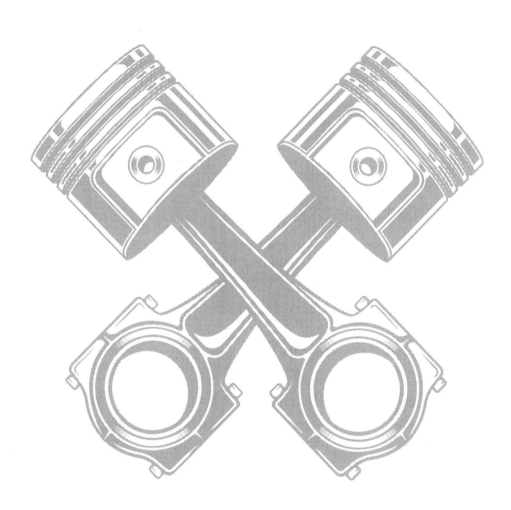

1972 Dodge Charger

1965 Ford Econoline

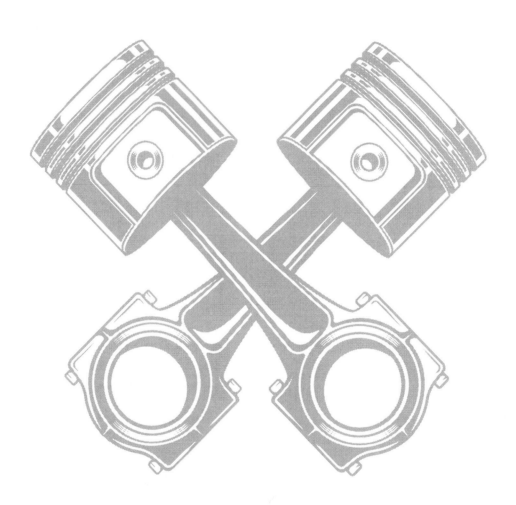

1951 Chevrolet Fleetline

1964 Pontiac GTO

1964 Jaguar E-Type

1941 Ford Pickup Hotrod

1966 Ford GT40

1972 VW Beetle

1950 Chevrolet Advance Design

1955 Chevrolet Corvette

1971 Plymouth Barracuda HEMI

1956 Chevrolet Hotrod

1947 Mercury Woodie Station Wagon

1968 Alfa Romeo Spider

1964 Pontiac Tempest GTO

1941 Willys MB Jeep

1957 Mercedes-Benz 300SL 'Gullwing'

1934 Packard Super Eight

1966 Lamborghini Miura

1969 Chevrolet Caprice

1940 Ford Deluxe Coupe

1965 Aston Martin DB5

1935 Ford Hotrod

1950 Dodge Power Wagon

1967 Chevrolet Camaro

1945 Dodge B Series

1965 Porsche 911

1959 Ford Thunderbird

1969 Pontiac Firebird Trans Am

1963 Chevrolet C/K

1965 Buick Riviera

1947 Studebaker Champion

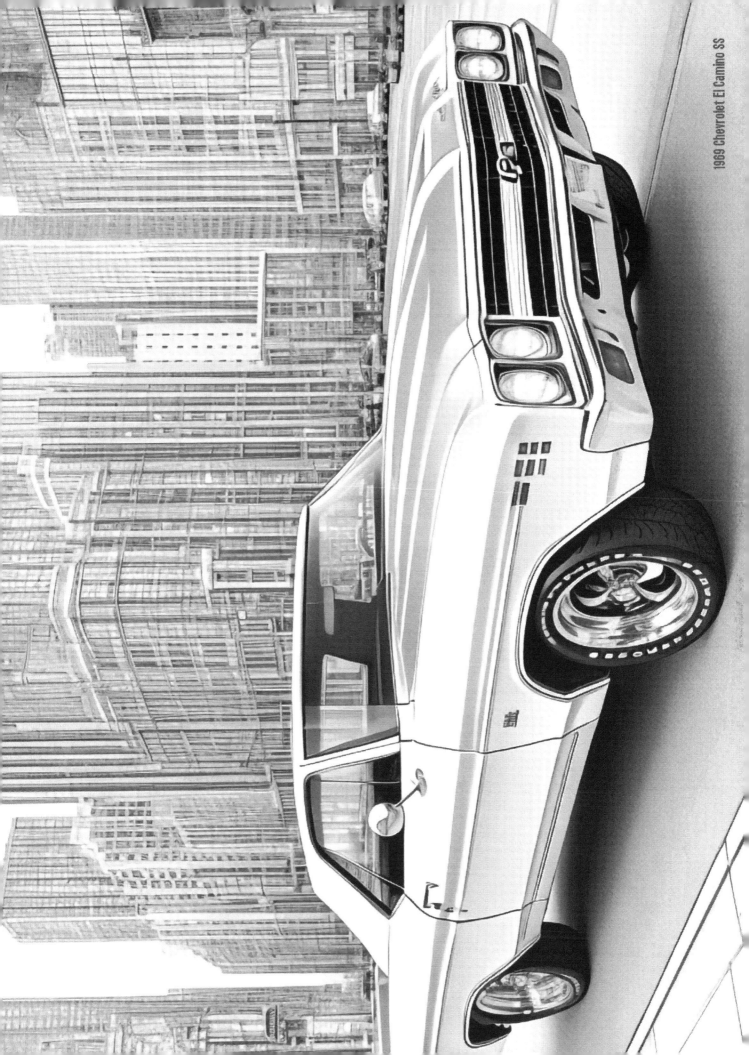

1969 Chevrolet El Camino SS

1965 Shelby Mustang GT350

1950 Ford F-Series

1963 Shelby Cobra

1964 Chevrolet Malibu SS

1959 Ford Ranchero

1938 Ford Hotrod

1955 Ford F-100

1969 Plymouth Road Runner

1969 Ford Bronoo

1959 Chevrolet Task Force

1963 Lincoln Continental

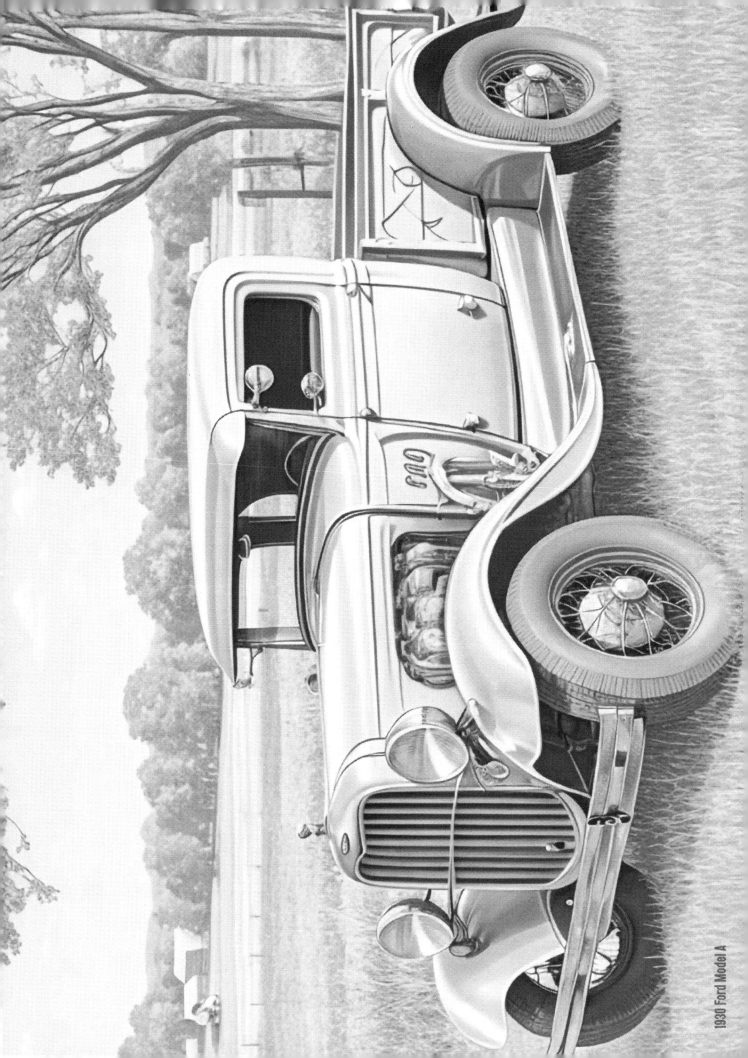

1930 Ford Model A

1969 Mercury Cougar Eliminator

Made in the USA
Columbia, SC
25 May 2024

36075533R00067